The Little Book of Positive Actions

that can move your life in big ways

T.A. Winter

BALBOA
PRESS

A DIVISION OF HAY HOUSE

Copyright © 2011 Theresa A. Winter

All rights reserved. No part of this book may be used or reproduced by any means, graphic, electronic, or mechanical, including photocopying, recording, taping or by any information storage retrieval system without the written permission of the publisher except in the case of brief quotations embodied in critical articles and reviews.

Balboa Press books may be ordered through booksellers or by contacting:

Balboa Press
A Division of Hay House
1663 Liberty Drive
Bloomington, IN 47403
www.balboapress.com
1-(877) 407-4847

Because of the dynamic nature of the Internet, any Web addresses or links contained in this book may have changed since publication and may no longer be valid. The views expressed in this work are solely those of the author and do not necessarily reflect the views of the publisher, and the publisher hereby disclaims any responsibility for them.

The author of this book does not dispense medical advice or prescribe the use of any technique as a form of treatment for physical, emotional, or medical problems without the advice of a physician, either directly or indirectly. The intent of the author is only to offer information of a general nature to help you in your quest for emotional and spiritual well-being. In the event you use any of the information in this book for yourself, which is your constitutional right, the author and the publisher assume no responsibility for your actions.

Any people depicted in stock imagery provided by Thinkstock are models, and such images are being used for illustrative purposes only. Certain stock imagery © Thinkstock.

ISBN: 978-1-4525-3194-6 (sc)
ISBN: 978-1-4525-3196-0 (dj)
ISBN: 978-1-4525-3195-3 (e)

Library of Congress Control Number: 2011902144

Printed in the United States of America
Balboa Press rev. date: 5/31/2011

"When we are in alignment with our purpose the whole Universe will roll at our feet in ecstasy."
- Kafka

Dedication

I dedicate this book to my beloved children, Kelly and August, (in no particular order). I could never have foreseen the impact each of you would have upon me. I am grateful for every moment, whether in laughter or in tears, that you have graced my life with your presence. I send you all my Love every single day.

I give thanks to my teachers who have directed, and my friends who supported my quest. No one travels this world alone, and I have been blessed with wonderful guidance and companionship. You all know who you are.

> I Am that which I become
> When I cease to be that
> Which I have been

I wake at dawn. The angle of the Sun's rays pierces the darkness. I lie still under cover and listen to my heart beating in the early morning shadows. As night is the day's companion, death is life's bride. She comes quietly to the altar, promising a new beginning, promising a new life. She is coy, shielded by a veil so that her face is hidden, but I wonder, is that a smile I see there. As the Sun rises we are called to the task of building this life, so that Death brings honor when the time arrives.

I reluctantly rise. I stare at the reflection in the mirror, and I see plainly that I have moved one day closer to death. I know this, not out of sadness or fear, but with an awareness of just how fragile is this vessel. As I move closer to death, I travel toward life, for in life we have a greater accessibility to our true self and its manifestations as Death releases us from illusion, allowing the reuniting and renewal of Spirit and self.

Contents

Foreword		xvii
One	*Find your Own Way*	1
Two	*Ask For What You Need and Want For Your Life*	9
Three	*Trust Your Intuition*	17
Four	*Be Prepared to Be Inspired Anytime, Anywhere*	25
Five	*Be Willing to Accept Direction from the Divine*	33
Six	*There is Holiness in Quiet Contemplation*	41
Seven	*Spend Time Every Day Improving Yourself*	49
Eight	*Let Go of the Need to be Right And Listen for a Change*	57
Nine	*That's Not Right For Me*	65
Ten	*A River Knows the Way*	73
Eleven	*Be Ever Mindful*	81
Twelve	*Be of Service*	89

*I'm going to shine my light
For everyone to see.
Not out of ego,
But for the Glory of Spirit
Who placed it there in me.*

Introduction

"Things do not change;
We change."
Henry David Thoreau

On November 11, 2008, my life changed forever. I was admitted to the emergency room at Lake Forest Hospital near Chicago. The doctor informed me that I had Chronic Myeloid Leukemia - CML. I never heard of it before, but would quickly come to know it well. I had not been in the hospital since my son was born over 17 years earlier. That had been a joyous occasion. This, not so much.

A normal white blood count is between 3.6 - 10 thousand. That day my white blood count was 271,000. It was not pleasant. As your white blood count approaches 300,000 it turns to sludge and tends to pool in your heart and brain; you are at serous risk of suffering heart attack or stroke. I was not in a good place. I was sick. I was scared. I felt lost.

I suggested to the oncologist that perhaps I could go home, get a good night's sleep and then return in the morning to begin treatment. A part of me knew that if he agreed, I would never return. He looked across the room at me, and without hesitation, in a tone I knew it was hopeless to argue with told me, "You're not going anywhere."

Nothing could have prepared me to make the phone call to my son from the hospital room. I wondered, where would the words come from to tell him I had Leukemia, but not let him know how frightened I was.

I was hooked up to an IV machine that I named "Bob". I was handed a lovely hospital gown (who designs these things?) to put on. I sat on the stiff bed, rested my head on the rubber sealed pillow, and cried. This was the last place I thought I would be.

Cancer is not a pretty picture and to protest my stay I refused to wash my hair until they sent me home. I sat wrapped in a blanket in the chair by the window in my hospital room looking out onto the parking lot where I knew my car was parked. I wanted to go home. I wanted to run away.

DANGER - DETOUR AHEAD! I had been going down the same path for years. Nothing awful but nothing amazing. I had once confided to someone that I wanted a life less ordinary, but one year blended aimlessly into another. Here I was, forced to make a sharp right turn, right into a new direction, right into a new life. I didn't want any part of it.

My son was going off to college the following year and I was afraid that I hadn't given him the wisdom that I wanted to share with him, lessons I had taken a lifetime to learn the hard way. What if the doctors were wrong. What if the "miracle drug" they were giving me didn't work and I wasn't going to be around when he embarked on his journey in life as an adult. What if I couldn't be there to guide and support him. My heart was aching.

I wanted him to know that if I didn't make it, if I couldn't be there to hug him, look into his eyes to tell him I loved him on graduation day, when he got married, or when his first child was born, that he was not alone. He would never be alone. In his heart I would always be with him, by his side, whispering in his ear, and watching over him.

Sometimes when fears cloud the words I wish to say, the angels bring them to me in my sleep, so that I may know them and hold them in my heart to share with others. Over the next several weeks after my diagnosis, I awoke in the early hours of the morning with words running through my mind like secret whispers from a friend. I scribbled them down on scraps of paper and went back to sleep. In the end, I found that there were twelve pieces of wisdom I was led to write down.

These are the lessons I wish to pass on to my son and to my daughter.

I hope that some few words in this little book have meaning for you, sustain you through times of challenge, and let you know in your heart that there is always hope, for you are truly never alone.

Author's Note

What is a labyrinth?

A labyrinth is a pattern with a single winding path that leads from the entrance to the center. There is only one way in and one way out; much like life itself.

Labyrinths have long been used as a tool for prayer and meditation. There is no wrong way to use a labyrinth, but it is best to begin by releasing your worries or concerns, so that when you reach the center you may be open to receive inspiration. On your journey back to the starting point you may relax and center yourself so that you bring the inspiration you received in the center back into your daily life.

The labyrinth you find in this book is a copy of the labyrinth I helped build at a healing and wellness organization in Wisconsin. You may use your finger or writing instrument to trace it for relaxation or reflection.

Writing in a journal is an excellent way to get in touch with your inner wisdom and highest self. Journal pages have been included at the end of each chapter to assist you in personal introspection. Allow your thoughts, feelings, and inspirations to flow freely through the pen and onto the page.

Foreword

*The trip of a thousand miles
begins with just one single step.
-Lao Tzu*

It may seem overwhelming to even think about making life changes. You're not certain you truly want to make a change, and you can't see the road ahead to where the changes may take you. Fear sets in. Have you ever experienced that dream where you are on a darkened staircase; you can't see more than one step ahead and you're afraid when you take the next step, it won't be there and you will fall into space.

Fear is part of our lives. We are hardwired to react to fear. On one level, it works to keep us safe from dangerous situations. It keeps us from crossing the expressway on foot during rush hour. Fear is to be respected but not allowed to be in charge, or it can freeze us in our tracks when the best thing for us is to move forward.

Living in fear is not living.

While we all yearn to make changes that we know will make us happy, it is important to have the courage and strength to take a step in the direction that will bring us out of the fear of our bad dream and into the light. It is really the small steps that add up and take us where we truly are meant to be headed.

To all who pick up this book. I send you healing prayers and best wishes at creating healthy change in your life, one step at a time. Know this, you will not only change your life, but everyone you meet will be transformed.

Love and Light,

Theresa

One

Find your Own Way

*"If a little dreaming is dangerous,
The cure for it is not to dream less,
But to dream more,
To dream all the time."*
Marcel Proust

Look in the mirror. Who are You? Not your title, earnings, or profession, not your role as parent, child, or sibling. Independent of all outside connections, do you know you? Do you understand who you are, what place you occupy in the space of your life?

Very often we become trapped in someone else's concept or image of who we are, what is acceptable or reasonable for us to reach, who we can become, or what heights we can attain. How often have we heard the word "No"? It was one of the first words we learned and it seems, more often than not, we skew our dreams and visions from others telling us, no it's not possible, or no, not yet - maybe in 10 or 20 years.

We become chained to the expectations of others. We become accustomed to the weight of those chains and forget the freedom of flight in our dreams. We worry if we don't do everything expected of us to make others happy, they may leave us. We worry we may be alone, unloved. We worry that we may be seen as selfish if we follow our dreams.

In reality, we are only tied by the chains which we allow to bind us. Don't keep your gifts a secret in your dreams. Live the dream of what it means to honestly be who you truly are. If it lives in your soul, then you must birth your dreams. This is your life. When you take your last breath, you want to honestly know that you lived the life of your dreams.

You are not a muddied puddle of water commonly seen and easily defined. You are an ocean of untapped possibility, of immense depth and breath, and intense power.

Get in touch with those dreams that live in your heart. Find the courage to live those dreams out loud. You may not be rich, but the richness of finding your own way will sustain you. Remember, when you are honestly living your dreams the Universe will provide you with what you need. Ask that the doors be open to you. The individuals who will support and assist you are on the other side of these doors waiting and smiling with open arms.

Journal

Journal

Journal

Journal

Two

Ask For What You Need and Want For Your Life

*"Knock and it shall be
opened unto you"*
Mathew 7:7

My father was a quiet man. He only gave me two pieces of advice:

#1 - If you are in a diner and there is only one piece of cake left, don't eat it; it's old. Ask for a piece of fresh cake. On the surface, this seems like pretty simple advice, but when you think about it, it really is sound advice about life - don't take whatever is left over. Ask for, and expect that you can have, what you want: the best. That may mean a fresh slice of triple chocolate cake or it may mean not allowing yourself to settle for something second rate. What is your heart's desire? Don't accept less.

#2 - My father told me, if there's something you want or need - ask; the worst someone can say is no and they may just say yes. We are so concerned about asking a question for fear of looking stupid.

How often do we get lost? Asking for directions can get us back on track. Sometimes our request for what we need is denied. Very often, but not always, the answer is yes.

Have the confidence to ask for help or assistance. There's nothing worse than not asking and finding out later that your request would have gladly been granted. It's your life. Don't just sit there and watch opportunities drift by.

Know yourself well enough to know what you need. Don't accept less, and when you need to, ask for help. No one else can read your mind. It is important to voice your wants and desires. When we express our Self to Spirit, we open ourselves to receive.

Journal

Journal

Journal

Journal

Three

Trust Your Intuition

*"No man can reveal to you
aught but that which already
lies half asleep in the dawning
of your knowledge."*
The Prophet

Intuition is a direct perception of your internal truth. Without effort, you reach inside yourself to touch the insight that patiently waits for you there.

Know when you are going against your true nature, your inner self. When it feels "wrong", somehow unsettling, it becomes hard work and requires extra energy. You have to sell yourself on the idea.

When you find yourself in this position, ask yourself, "Is this what I really want to be doing? Is this where I truly belong?" Quiet your mind, center yourself in your heart, and know that the heart never lies. Listen and the answer will come to you quietly. You may be tempted to debate the answer - don't. Accept that your inner self has communicated with you for your highest good.

You may want to ask others for their opinion, to hear their advice for you. That's fine, if it helps you settle in your heart where you need to be, but remember you know yourself better than anyone .

Intuition is a sacred journey you take with yourself to the center of your being. It requires a path paved with faith. Open completely to your knowledge. There is a diamond at the center of your being that is pure beauty and knowledge which lights your way. Unearth that diamond and watch it sparkle in the sun light.

That brilliance is you.

Journal

Journal

Journal

Journal

Four

*Be Prepared
to Be Inspired
Anytime, Anywhere*

"The sense of wonder, that is the sixth sense."
D. H. Lawrence

Stay open to the arrival of new experiences and allow yourself the possibility for change and the probability for growth. Our purpose in life is to be a vessel open for beautiful things to fill us up. When we get stuck in the rut of making more money and being attached to accruing more things we become toxic and nothing can grow in us.

Sometimes we are looking for a dramatic sign, the Red Sea to part, or winning the big Lotto to believe our lives can take a dramatic change for the better. Wake up! I'm talking about finding the miracle in the butterfly that flitters past you. Butterflies don't seem that amazing to you? Did you know that the caterpillar turns into a type of primordial ooze in the cocoon, then reconfigures into a butterfly before it emerges. Amazing!

Do one new thing each month. It could be as simple as going home by a previously unexplored route, even if you hit a dead end, you have been someplace new that day. Try on clothes that you would never wear in public, just to see how you look in the mirror in a new skin. Go to a movie or out to dinner by yourself, just to see what kind of company you really are. Plan an exotic vacation that you may or may never take, just to imagine the thrill of adventure. Make eye contact with a stranger at the coffee shop and say hello, just to connect with another.

Just beyond your comfort zone is growth, learning, and enlightenment. You will never know what you may learn unless you wonder.

Journal

Journal

Journal

Journal

Five

Be Willing to Accept Direction from the Divine

"The most wonderful aspect of the universe is the direction of free beings under Divine guidance."
-Joseph De Maistre

Divine presence surrounds us, from the crocuses bursting through the spring snow, to the stranger who stops to help you change a flat tire, to the Labrador Retriever who gazes up at you with total love and shows you what joy there is in living an honorable life. We merely need to look around and truly see what is waiting to be discovered. Take a moment from your cocoon of self-involvement to see what is right in front of your eyes. There is an ever constant presence of Divine Spirit. It is an open door to the possibility of comfort, love, and growth.

You may ask, what about the murder, war, tragedies that we read about in the newspaper and see on TV. There is much heartache in the world, but there is constant love and assistance from Divine Source available if we seek out the grace.

Divine direction is always available, but often our eyes are blinded by our own self-importance, our ears are deafened by our fears.

Each day close your eyes, be grateful for that day, for the opportunities you experience in your life. As for the days you regard as really bad, be even more grateful because those challenges help you grow, develop, and rise above difficulties or obstacles. You didn't do it alone. You are never alone. You are being watched over and guided. Listen to the guidance and demonstrate gratitude. On those bad days, you can be even more grateful you made it through.

Close your eyes and feel your heart. Feel it beat in your chest, without your direction or even asking it to. Feel the power of your breath fill your lungs. This is a beautiful thing. This is just the beginning of Divine direction

Say thank you. Feel warmth in your heart as the love and gratitude grows from that simple gesture.

Now open your eyes and see the world differently. The love in your heart is spreading from your chest throughout your entire body and it changes you. Extend that warmth to others in your family, the cashier at the grocery store, the guy in the car who just cut you off.

You cannot do this all on your own. You cannot find your way traveling by your volition alone. Direction from the Divine travels from the heart and Spirit to guide you. It will direct your feet on the path of love and compassion. The student always walks behind the teacher, is quiet when the teacher gives instructions, and looks to the teacher as an example of right thought, right speech, and right actions. Embrace the Divine as your teacher.

Journal

Journal

Journal

Journal

Six

There is Holiness in Quiet Contemplation

*"In cultivating your mind know how to dive
in the hidden depths"*
- Lao Tzu

We read self-help books, watch videos, and go to lectures to find out the secret of being happy, thin, successful, or abundant. But the greatest changes occur when you simply open up to the beauty within you. We are most often 5% who we truly are and 95% comprised of reactions to our interpretation of our perception. We can find the larger portion of who we truly are when we take the time to look and listen. In the silence of meditation the real you is allowed to step forward. Get to know you.

Every day, make time to be alone for quiet contemplation, to explore who you are down to the very last cell in your body. Allow your imagination the freedom to soar where you dare not go in your every day reality, and to connect to the essence of the Spirit which resides in your heart. Make time now to sit alone and allow your higher self to rise to the surface. You will be pleasantly surprised at how truly amazing you are.

You may feel you don't have time to sit still. Who has time heading off to work, preparing for tests, and trying to remove gum from the bottom of your shoe - you don't even have the energy to find out how it got there in the first place. The hectic pace of your life is not going to change until you make your personal peace a priority. Life will still be hectic, but your attachment to it will not command your attention.

It is a commitment you make to your life. It is an act of love you give to yourself. Dive deep into the whirlpool of your life and find yourself in the very center, still and calm.

Get to know you.

Journal

Journal

Journal

Journal

Seven

*Spend Time Every
Day Improving Yourself*

*"The unexamined life
is not worth living"*
- Socrates

Do you know why New Year's resolutions usually fail? Because they were not born of your heart's true wishes. I believe that it is everyone's sacred responsibility in this lifetime to truly know themselves. Make no mistake about it, it is hard work to truly get honest with yourself. Only in knowing our self can we discover how we can help and serve others. Only by helping and serving others can we thrive. You have a responsibility to yourself and everyone in your life to be the best you can be.

Start today. Shut off the TV. Put down the Ipod. Read books that stimulate your mind. Write your thoughts and feelings in a journal. Most importantly, talk with people, especially those you love and those who inspire you.

We all know about the reports on exercise and eating healthy, but still we over indulge and we waddle around with sagging butts and beer guts. This body is a gift, but if we don't take proper care of it, it can be recalled. Do something physical every day, starting with just a walk around the block. Cut out the junk food and stop thinking it's cool to drink alcohol every day. It's not.

Your life is created from what you put your attention on. If you put your attention on love, peace, and compassion then that is who you are. If you put your attention on anger, resentment, or fear then that is who you will be. Your choice. No blaming. You choose today, right now. Who do you want to be?

You can change your life by changing the vision you hold of who you are. Change the vision you hold of yourself by committing to be the highest ideal of yourself, every single day.

Who would you like to be?

Journal

Journal

Journal

Journal

Eight

*Let Go of the Need
to be Right
And Listen for a Change*

"The first duty of love is to listen"
- Paul Tillich

This is a very competitive society; those who come out on top are viewed as successful and powerful. We want to be right, know the right answer, buy the right stock, go to the right school, take the right job, marry the right person. If we aren't right , then we have made a mistake, and our chances at happiness are a bit tenuous. That's a lot of pressure, this need we have to be right.

It is more than just a fear of being seen as less than powerful or infallible. There is a fear that if we are not right, then we will be vulnerable to those who are right and lose our power. They will then hold this power over us.

We don't realize that when we enter into life as a competition we shut ourselves off to the possibility of acquiring new information, or learning new lessons which assist in our goal of self-evolvement. We stifle our own growth as we try to control others.

When someone begins to tell you something, especially surrounding a subject you have a strong opinion, you stop listening almost immediately and begin to formulate your response. If the person is lucky, you may actually wait until they are finished before you promote your case for being right.

When we allow others the right to their opinion instead of trying to win them over to our point of view, we leave a space for our own growth and self-discovery. We afford them respect and dignity for their individuality.

Listening is an act of love we both give and receive.

Today, listen carefully to the opinion of someone else, even if you disagree with it. Understand you are not vulnerable if someone else is able to hold their own opinion or values, and be very aware that not interrupting is NOT equivalent to listening.

When you argue with someone you struggle over the energy to be the winner - defeating the other. While we can justify, even enjoy, the battle we wage, our hearts are torn and suffer from our lack of love and compassion toward another. We may try to justify to others that our judgments are righteous, and we may even convince them of the validity of our point of view, but still we are really just trying to come out on top. No one is the winner there.

Make a mental note during the next few days of how often we shut people down without even giving them a chance to state their opinion or tell their story. How often does this happen to you? How does the other person react when you allow them the opportunity to "find their own voice" without you enforcing your own beliefs? How does it feel to give someone else the opportunity to know that they are being heard and seen?

We can hold personal freedom in the midst of differing opinions while respecting ourselves and others. We can live in an atmosphere of communion without losing ourselves.

Listen. Learn. Love.

Journal

Journal

Journal

Nine

That's Not Right For Me

*"Never violate the sacredness of
your individual self-respect"
- Theophile Goutier*

Much of our time is spent feeling isolated, rejected, and abandoned because we believe the people around us do not see and value us for who we truly are. We find ourselves doing things we are not comfortable with in the hopes of feeling valued, loved, and accepted. Only suffering can come from our willingness to forsake our commitment to ourselves in order to "fit in". We do not fully realize our inherent value and do not set boundaries or limits.

Boundaries are how far we are willing to let someone into our life while still maintaining our personal comfort and integrity. Limits are what we are willing and comfortable doing for someone else; how far we will go, regardless of what we hope to get in return from them.

Boundaries and limits are highly individual and may fluctuate over time. No one however will stand up for you until you stand up for yourself. First give some honest consideration to the motives behind your actions. Ask yourself, what is the intention driving you. Is it honest? Is it honorable?

When you have a good idea about what is and isn't acceptable to you, it is time to practice one simple phrase: "That's not right for me."

This one simple statement carries weight. Friends, family, or the boss may not hear, or believe that you are sincere the first few times you say this. Truly, do not expect them to pat you on the back because they are no longer able to manipulate you. Be honest with yourself, determine your boundaries, and set your limits. Then, stand up for yourself - because if you don't no one else will.

Respect yourself.

Journal

Journal

Journal

Journal

Ten

A River Knows the Way

*"The best and most beautiful things cannot be
seen or touched
- they must be felt with the heart."
- Helen Keller*

Forgive yourself for not being who you are today ten years ago. Read that sentence again.

Education comes in stages. We go to kindergarten before we can go to college. When we get to college and experience a higher level of learning, we don't beat ourselves up for not knowing when we were five, so why do we beat ourselves up for not being further along in our education in life. It was necessary to learn the lessons five or ten years ago so that we could be at this stage of learning we are at today. Go easy on yourself. You wouldn't be angry at your ten year old for not knowing trigonometry.

Like the river, there is something moving through us. Anyone who has ever stood on a bridge and watched the movement of a river has experienced first hand that there is a river moving inside the river. It is where the current moves effortlessly, faster, and uninhibited.

There is this river moving through you. To find this place makes the journey easier. You move through your life with less effort, fewer obstacles. With experience you learn to read the signs of the life, so your understanding grows and you become more fluid.

That is the rhythm of the heart. When we think, feel, and speak from the heart we find a path inside our lives which makes learning and understanding smoother and more effortless. Just as the river changes in depth and breadth as it flows, so does our life. Learning and understanding comes in the flow and direction of the currents. As they shift our perspective changes and our view of life develops.

Sit quietly alone in a room. Take several deep breaths and let the day flow off you like rain off the treetops. Form a picture in your mind as if you are sitting in a movie theater. This movie features you ten years ago. It may be painful to watch yourself make all those old mistakes, caught up in the old patterns, but hang in there and breath. Feel the joy, the pain, the uncertainty, and the fear.

This is the old you, and although you have a connection to this old sense of self, you can maintain an impartial distance or detachment while holding a place of compassion.

Now split the screen and see yourself as you are today. Value the effort you have put in to becoming this evolved version of yourself. Feel an acceptance and understanding for whom you once were. The choices you made, may not have been truly in your best interest, but it was the best you could do with the information you had at the time.

Confirm for the old you that you will learn and grow, and life will flow. Let the old you know that there is hope. Hope is the most important thing for our spirits to hold onto; without hope we are like the river dried up from drought.

Hope cannot be seen or touched but moves through the heart to strengthen us. Even though it is invisible, it flows like a river inside our body, mind, and spirit.

Journal

Journal

Journal

Eleven

Be Ever Mindful

"Just relax, breathe, and feel"
- gt

We rush through our lives to the point where each day spins past us. As we twirl tighter we lose track of who we are. The adrenaline becomes addictive, but masks our ability to just be. When we slow down to experience life, we begin to feel what it means to be alive.

Be mindful of how you move through your day. Being mindful allows us the capability to affect and transform who we are, how we conduct ourselves, and how we create our life. Mindfulness brings us to an awakened state of being as we move through the moments of our life.

Mindfulness Exercises:

Breathing:

Do you find yourself yawning in the middle of the afternoon? Instead of reaching for the cup of coffee, sit quietly for two minutes and monitor your breathing. Breath in through your nose, up toward your eyes and out through your mouth. Feel your lungs expand and then slowly release your breath. You begin to float on this cushion of air. Just remember to come back down; you've still got work to do. Do it with a sense of mindfulness of your place in this world.

Walking

This is not your average walking where the goal is to get from point A to point B as quickly as you can. Step forward, being conscious of your heel as it touches the ground, then the sole, and the ball of your foot until finally you feel the toes touching. With your foot now firmly planted on the ground, slowly raise up your other foot and move it forward to repeat the first step.

Feel each movement of your body through time and space. This mindful walking practice aids in keeping us grounded and is a very nice massage for Mother Earth. And if you do it in your backyard, it will surely give the neighbors something to talk about.

Eating:

We pull through the drive-up at a fast food restaurant, pull into a spot in the parking lot and stuff the food into our mouth as fast as possible. Do we even taste what we are eating?

The food we consume each day is the fuel our body needs to get through life, but it is also a source of emotional and spiritual nourishment. If our only object was to sustain life, we could gnaw on wafer supplements, but we have been blessed with senses that need to be nurtured and enlivened to fully satisfy our soul as well as our stomachs.

Be conscious of the foods you choose to put in your body, how your body reacts to those foods, why you eat, and who you share your meals with. Look at your food, chew slowly, put your fork down between bites. Don't watch television - have a conversation.

Relax and have an experience.

Journal

Journal

Journal

Twelve

Be of Service

"The fragrance always remains on the hand that gives the rose"
- Gandhi

What I can tell you for certain is that this life is a tool for learning about yourself, the Spirit that moves within you, and your birthright to the greatness that is your destiny. In order to access this knowledge you must be of service to others. To be of service is a virtue that opens the heart of those who give and of those who receive. To act toward the betterment of humanity is like the arrow of life finding its mark at the center of the target, it is a path that is straight and true.

Opportunities are placed before us everyday for our consideration; the homeless, the battered, and the defenseless look to us to be seen, search our faces to be recognized, and reach out to be held in our embrace. Do not turn away. If one person suffers, true happiness and contentment cannot be fully attained.

By being of service to others, we come to a better understanding of who we are and of our place in this lifetime to create a divine existence for our self and others. It could take the form of donating money to a charity, reading to an elderly person, helping build homes for the needy. You will know it is the right thing to do in your heart. Don't let that opportunity slip away.

Be of service, to the attunement of your spirit and the enrichment in the life of another. Small acts of kindness never go unnoticed, by those who have received the kindness and of your own heart which yearns to be seen, heard, and touched.

Journal

Journal

Journal

*Stand tall upon Mother Earth
Blessed by the warmth of
Father Sky.
And know in your heart you are worthy
And held precious by the Universe.
That is all you truly need.*

I give you this one thought to keep
I am with you still - I do not sleep
I am a thousand winds that blow,
I am the diamond glints on snow.

I am the sunlight on ripened grain,
I am the gentle autumn rain,
When you awaken in the morning's hush
I am the swift, up lifting rush
Of quiet birds in circled flight.
I am the soft stars that shine at night.

Do not think of me as gone -
I am with you still - in each new dawn

Native American Prayer

A portion of all proceeds of this book are donated to the Cancer Wellness Center, Northbrook, IL for their amazing work in meeting the needs of the cancer patient, family, friends, and care givers.

Special thanks to Howard Lewis and the Family Heritage group for their continuing support throughout my cancer challenge. Cancer may have changed my life, but you provided hope to me and my son for the future. May all of you at Family Heritage be blessed with continued success in your mission of Destiny, Devotion, and Dedication. Many thanks!

www.ingramcontent.com/pod-product-compliance
Lightning Source LLC
Chambersburg PA
CBHW020011050426
42450CB00005B/415